CHARLES ROSNER

FIGHTING SHIPS OF THE U.S.A.

A Battleship Is the Mightiest Fighting Machine Yet Invented by Man

FIGHTING SHIPS
OF THE U.S.A.

By LIEUTENANT VICTOR F. BLAKESLEE

ILLUSTRATED BY CHARLES ROSNER

WITH AN INTRODUCTION BY ADMIRAL WILLIAM V. PRATT

RANDOM HOUSE · NEW YORK

Acknowledgment

The author and publishers wish to express their appreciation to the Navy Department for much of the source material used in this book, and to Lieutenant Wilson Starbuck, U. S. Naval Reserve, for his advice concerning the artist's paintings.

CONTENTS

INTRODUCTION BY ADMIRAL WILLIAM V. PRATT

AFTER every major war that our country has fought, the United States Navy has been allowed to decline in strength. This was true after 1814, after the War between the States, and more recently after the world holocaust of 1914-1918. In 1916 the United States laid down the greatest naval building program known to maritime history — and in 1922 we scrapped most of that program. Thus whenever our country has been faced with a serious emergency, our Navy has had to build new ships and train new men quickly.

Today we are again faced with a national emergency — this time in both oceans. We are building up the Navy at top speed. This enormous program will not, however, be completed before 1945 or 1946, since we cannot build battleships — nor, indeed, thousands of planes — overnight. But war can come overnight. Our Navy must therefore be ready to fight with the ships and planes it has available when war begins, not with a building program completed after war ends.

Today we are confronted by the fact that our wide oceans are no longer barriers against possible invasion. As a consequence, our people are coming to the realization that an adequate Navy in time of peace becomes our richest asset in time of war.

Were I to be asked what the future of our country most depends upon, I would say, "An ever more powerful Navy — above, on, and under the sea — a Navy capable of meeting, even in peacetime, all possible combinations of enemies at least on equal terms."

Every citizen today should know his country's Navy, which is the equal of any other in the world and of which all Americans can be proud. Lieutenant Blakeslee has therefore done a patriotic service in describing for us, out of his own experience as a naval officer, the ships and planes and men that defend our shores.

Let us always keep our Navy strong. Then we need never worry about our ability to defend our country and the many liberties that we hold dear.

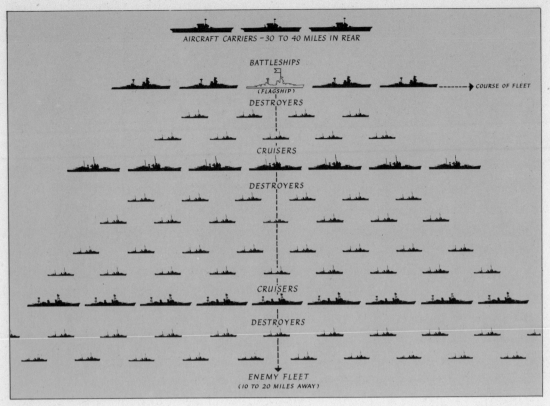

The United States Fleet Takes up a Formation Like This in Practice Maneuvers When Making Ready for Battle with the Enemy Fleet

1 THE UNITED STATES FLEET

INTO the silver haze of early morning steams the United States Fleet, most powerful armada afloat. The mighty prows of a hundred ships cut through the still waters, leaving in their wakes foaming maelstroms. On they go proudly to sea, the great battleships, aircraft carriers, and cruisers, flanked by sleek destroyers and sinister submarines, while overhead drone shore-based planes, occasionally breaking into a whirring roar as they swoop low in flight maneuvers over the steel caravan of ships.

According to Navy tradition, the flagship of the Commander-in-Chief leads the long line, his four-starred blue flag straining at the mainmast as the engine-room telegraph rings up standard speed. The signal bridge is alive with activity. Swift-moving quartermasters are "bending on" pennants, while flag-hoist men run them up to the yardarm. "Take it away!" shouts the chief signalman, naming in order the flags to be used.

On the bridges of other ships, binoculars and telescopes, with straining eyes behind them, pick up the signal, and the same signal is hoisted in acknowledgment, until all ships have answered. "Execute!" comes the order from the flagship's bridge. Then the flag-hoists all come down together, and the fleet changes course to starboard.

On and on into the path of the rising sun, toward the enemy fleet, steams America's first line of defense, every officer and man alert for the stern business that lies ahead. Fleet Problems must be worked out — secret maneuvers and battle practice in imitation of a real fight at sea. For without training Uncle Sam's Navy would be worthless should a real enemy attack our shores to clear the way for an invasion.

On the battleships, turret crews are now manning the 14-inch guns, and other highly trained men the 5-inch broadside batteries. High-pressure boilers produce the power for full speed ahead on all engines, and every man jack is at his post of general quarters, eager to carry out his assignment. In a wide screen about the battleships are cruisers, destroyers, and submarines, ready to strike the first blows at the enemy and to protect the big "battle wagons" against enemy submarines and destroyers with their torpedoes. Meanwhile, far away, planes of the fleet are engaging hostile aircraft and radioing in the positions of enemy ships.

Now the battleships come within range of the enemy, and with their long-range guns begin to speak thunderously. The booming of the guns, hurling tons of metal and high explosives at every salvo, is heard for a hundred miles along the coast as deadly projectiles smash into the enemy fleet at a range of 35,000 yards, almost 20 miles.

As the fleets close for the combat, all the resources of the modern naval force — battleships, cruisers, destroyers, submarines, aircraft — go into deadly action with their shells, torpedoes, bombs, and depth charges.

But this, after all, is a sham battle — a battle to test the mettle of our Navy. When the smoke has cleared away, umpires figure out the scores of the opposing fleets, determining which ships theoretically have been hit or sunk, how many planes have spun broken into the sea, and which side in the mock fight has been victorious. This modern naval engagement may have lasted a bare half hour. The winner has been the side which hit first and fastest from the farthest distance. Minutes and seconds have been more valuable than diamonds and rubies; the failure of one man to do his job might have meant disaster to the victor.

The battle has been won by equipment, skill, and courage. The fleet is literally a mass of machinery designed to carry explosives and, allowing for speed, direction, wind, and other factors, to discharge these explosives accurately at an enemy.

The men who operate this great collection of seagoing machinery are highly skilled specialists who know exactly how and when to do their jobs. But, more than this, they have the spirit of those tars who, in the days of John Paul Jones, fought sea battles at point-blank range, often boarding the enemy after coming alongside and making fast to him with grappling hooks. These modern Navy men, with the finest naval equipment in the world, are prepared for every emergency, watching over the security of the United States day and night so that 130,000,000 free people may go about the business of life in peace.

The Arms of the Fleet

The ships of our Navy with their officers and crews are known as the United States Fleet. This great collection of seagoing men and guns, the most powerful afloat today, is divided into three smaller fleets which guard us in the Pacific and Atlantic Oceans.

At the head of each fleet is a four-star admiral, the admiral of the Pacific Fleet being also commander-in-chief of the United States Fleet. Each admiral has his staff

A Battleship of the *Texas* Class Dashes off on a Mission

Country	BATTLESHIPS	AIRCRAFT CARRIERS	CRUISERS	DESTROYERS	SUBMARINES
UNITED STATES Totals-	15 / 17 / 32	6 / 12 / 18	37 / 54 / 91	159 / 205 / 364	106 / 79 / 185
GREAT BRITAIN Totals-	16 / 7 / 23	8 / 4 / 12	66 / 18* / 84*	233 / 3* / 236*	45
GERMANY Totals-	4 / 2 / 6	1 / 1 / 2	9 / 6 / 15	47* / UNKNOWN / UNKNOWN	120* / 180* / 300*
JAPAN Totals-	10 / 8* / 18*	8 / 2 / 10	46 / 10 / 56	125 / 11 / 136	71 / 7 / 78
ITALY Totals-	3 / 2 / 5	NONE / NONE / NONE	15 / 14 / 29	115 / 12 / 127	92* / 16 / 108*
RUSSIA Totals-	3 / 3 / 6	NONE / 2 / 2	9 / 4 / 13	64 / 34* / 98*	171* / UNKNOWN / UNKNOWN
FRANCE Totals-	1 / 4 / 5	1 / 2 / 3	14 / 3 / 17	50* / 30* / 80*	60* / 22 / 82*

STRENGTHS OF FLEETS OF VARIOUS COUNTRIES.   Black Ships Represent Ships Built; White Ships, Ships Building

*Estimated.

of experts in gunnery, strategy, and engineering, with vice admirals and rear admirals controlling the battleship, cruiser, destroyer, and submarine forces.

The Asiatic Fleet, the smallest of the three, protects Americans and American property in the Far East — in the vicinity of China, Japan, the Philippine Islands, and other places in the Orient. This small but swift little fleet is made up mostly of destroyers and submarines, which can speed quickly to the scene of any trouble. Also in the Asiatic Fleet are the gunboats which steam up and down the Yangtze River in China, looking out for the safety of Americans and their belongings in that war-torn land.

The Pacific Fleet keeps watch on the rest of the Pacific Ocean from Alaska to the Hawaiian Islands and southward. The Pacific Fleet could dash to the aid of its smaller brother, the Asiatic Fleet, if necessary, but its main job is to see that no enemy could get near to our Pacific Coast or the Panama Canal without being sunk. In time of war, ships in the Pacific could slip through the Panama Canal to aid an embattled fleet in the Atlantic.

The Atlantic Fleet, the third main part of the Navy, is the watchdog of our eastern shores. With its guns, planes, and torpedoes, all handled by skillful and determined men, it is always ready to resist any attack across the Atlantic Ocean. Like the Pacific Fleet, in wartime it could hurry through the Panama Canal to help our ships in the other ocean.

One important job that the Pacific and Atlantic Fleets are now doing is the patrolling of the Neutrality Zones in the Western Hemisphere. Since many foreign warships are now on the oceans looking for enemy craft to destroy, it is important for the United States to keep order in North and South American waters, so that our merchant ships will be safe. The warring countries have been informed by our government that our Navy intends to prevent fighting in these waters, which are strips of ocean bordering the shores of South, Central, and North America. Here day by day, hour by hour, our warships and submarines are on the alert, determined to keep war as far away from our shores as possible.

The Navy Looks Ahead

Because of the wars in Europe and Asia, the Navy is now being rapidly enlarged so that it can hold off any enemy or combination of enemies attacking across either the Pacific or the Atlantic. Our shipyards are running full time, turning out new battleships, destroyers, submarines, and other engines of destruction. Airplane factories are booming. New men are being trained rapidly so that the new ships will not lack officers and crews. Our naval strategists are working out defense plans, so

Torpedo Planes Like These, with Their Deadly "Fish," Are Always a Serious Menace to an Enemy Fleet

CHARLES ROSNER

that in case of emergency the ships we have in any danger zone could be quickly reinforced and strike any enemy hard before he gained a foothold on our shores.

Careful, long-range planning and up-to-date weapons: these are the watchwords in our seagoing forces today.

Modern transportation, the airplane, and radio communication have brought the six continents of the world closer together than ever before. This means that our Navy must be more alert than at any other time in our history — ready to throw back attacks from any direction. The Navy must always respond to change, adopt new methods and new inventions, and organize itself in new ways in order to keep well ahead of other navies.

Who of us knows what the world will be like ten years from now? Tanks may become as large as battleships; airplanes may carry 700 men instead of 70 and be able to transport huge cargoes across the seas and over the land, as do ocean liners and railroads today. There will be new kinds of ships, submarines, mines, torpedoes, seagoing airplanes, and other weapons. These are just a few of the things that the Navy must think about and plan for night and day.

Keeping in Practice

But the Navy must do more than plan and keep up with new inventions and build more ships. Every man in our sea forces must be kept in practice so that he would be ready to do his job quickly and efficiently if an enemy fleet appeared on our horizons.

Each year one of the Navy's big bills is the bill for ammunition, and the money is well spent. Men cannot be trained to fire guns, discharge torpedoes, and drop bombs squarely on targets without plenty of practice. The fleet therefore has frequent battle practices, either on a vast scale with hundreds of ships, or with fewer ships, divided into "friendly" and "hostile" forces. In this way every man learns how to do his work as he would do it under battle conditions. Gunners get the chance to blow holes in floating or aerial targets miles away, and torpedomen practice shooting dummy "fish," as torpedoes are called, against other ships. At sea and ashore Navy airmen keep in practice by bombing and machine-gunning and torpedoing old hulks or other targets. The ammunition used in all this practice costs a great deal of money, but the Navy must know its job.

Friendly competition between the men and ships is so keen that the average performance is very high. Turret crews are determined to win the "Efficiency E" by making more hits in less time than any other turret on the ship. Squadrons on the aircraft carriers do their best to excel one another in dogfighting, scouting, bombing, and other operations. The men on each destroyer try to "sink" more submarines than any others. The navigators on each ship are on their toes to outmaneuver the "enemy" so that he will be at a disadvantage. The engineering departments labor hard to win the efficiency "White E." And so with every man and group of men in the fleet.

This competition, keen though it is, does not mean that in the Navy it is every man for himself or every ship for itself. The men and ships are a hard-working team; every officer and man must work for the Navy as a whole. Only a naval force in which every man and every ship can do the assigned job fast and well can claim the title of our First Line of Defense.

Patrol Planes Such as This, Shown over a Group of Destroyers, Can Fly 3,000 Miles in Their Task of Guarding Our Coasts and Bases against Any Surprise Enemy Attack

This Heavy Cruiser Is Part of the Backbone of the Fleet

2 THE BACKBONE OF THE FLEET

BACKBONE of the fleet are the battleships and cruisers. These iron monsters, up to 35,000 tons in weight (or "displacement"), stand between America and all who would threaten us with attack by sea. Today our main battle line consists of fifteen battleships, supported by thirty-seven modern cruisers. The two-ocean Navy now being built will have thirty-two American battleships — more than any other nation — and ninety-one cruisers.

The "Battle Wagons"

The battleship is the biggest combination of striking power and protective armament afloat. It is designed to give enormous punishment and to withstand terrific pounding. Its sides are covered with heavy armor plate; its main battery of guns — those in the big revolving turrets — are the most powerful in the world. In addition to these long-range "rifles," the battleship has a secondary battery along its sides. These are smaller guns for shorter ranges, to be used against enemy destroyers and submarines that might get by the protective screen of cruisers and destroyers. On deck are many rapid-fire guns to give hostile aircraft a hot reception.

Battleships make good targets for torpedoes. Hence, naval architects have designed them with many watertight compartments. If any compartments are struck by torpedoes, the others will probably keep the ship afloat. At least five torpedoes, striking a ship at strategic points, would be necessary to put her out of action. This additional protection, combined with its armament, makes the battleship the most important member of the fleet. Though many people argue that the battleship is outmoded, too expensive and too big, the proud "battle wagon" still rules the waves, and with its long cruising radius and staying power will undoubtedly maintain its first-line position at sea for many years to come.

A Sailor's Life

A battleship is not all machinery, guns, and armor plate. Equally important is its soul, its driving force, embodied in 1,500 men. Every man on the ship is important in his own right, from the captain down to the second-class water tenders — the men who see that the boilers get plenty to drink. Without this spirit, the battleship would be a lifeless, clumsy mass of steel.

Life aboard begins at sun-up. There are boats to be rigged, decks to be swabbed, and other jobs to be done according to the executive officer's morning order book. A half hour before reveille the boatswain's mates, hammock stowers, and masters-at-arms are called. They wake the crew and see that every man turns out promptly. Hammocks are "stowed," or folded and put away; cots and bedding are made up. Reveille sounds at 5:30 on the bugle and boatswain's pipe. Coffee is served, and the day's work begins. Decks are wet down; brasswork is shined and paintwork is scrubbed. Then to breakfast.

Sailors Eat

These days sailors don't have to eat hardtack and water and beans for every meal. Modern kitchens and up-to-date refrigeration plants give Uncle Sam's seamen the best of fresh, carefully prepared foodstuffs. When "mess gear," or kitchen duty, is sounded at 7:15, men assigned to that duty go to the ship's galley for "chow." Usually one man is given two tables to prepare and serves twenty of his shipmates. At 7:30 the entire crew is at the piping-hot breakfast.

At 8 o'clock the engineers, or "black gang," fall in for "quarters," which is the call to their posts. The band plays the "Star-Spangled Banner," and Old Glory is hoisted. Band practice continues from 8:00 to 8:30, as the deck force "turns to" on

20

tasks about the ship. Sick call is at 8:05, and all men ill report to "sick bay," the ship's infirmary, for medical examination. At 8:45 the men "lay below" to clean up for inspection.

Quarters for the muster of the deck force comes at 9:00 and is followed by setting-up exercises, for at sea, in the close confines of a ship, the men's physical condition must be kept in the pink. At 9:30 drill call, or general quarters, is sounded, and all men go to their battle stations.

Morning hours are filled with drills at guns, boat drills, and fire, man-overboard, or collision drills. After 10:30 there is usually an hour's instruction period, so that every man will know his job thoroughly and have a chance to prepare for promotion.

Routine in port and at sea is much the same. At 11:30 usually the crew "knocks off" work, and chow is "piped down," or announced, at 12:00. The band plays again for lunch, and at 1:00 the men are back at work. They quit for the day at 3:45 to indulge in afternoon sports and other recreations.

A Fighting Plane Takes off from an Aircraft Carrier While the "Asbestos Man," So Called Because of His Asbestos Suit, Stands by to Help If Any Plane in Landing Should Crash and Catch Fire

Giant Searchlights Probe the Skies for Enemy Raiders

Sailors Can Play

The Navy has found that play is as necessary as work. Every ship has its football team, its basketball and baseball teams, its boxing and wrestling bouts. Competition with other ships develops a spirit of friendly rivalry. The latest movies are shown, often before people see them in large theaters ashore. Backgammon boards, too, are well used, for the old sailor's game of acey-deucy is still popular. In boat races and other sports, including sailing, various ships compete for prizes as enthusiastically as they strive for excellence in engineering and gunnery.

A Man's Home

A battleship is a man's home. It contains libraries with up-to-date books on many subjects. There are chaplains to carry on church and welfare activities, and committees to provide entertainment. Nor are the welfare activities limited to the ships. Twenty-five years ago the battleship *New York* began the custom of providing a Christmas party for poor and crippled children in the port where it happened to be during the holiday season. Now with large ships this custom is almost universal.

Aboard a battleship lifelong friendships are made. To be sure, there are courts-martial and quarrels and jealousies; but heroism and fun and comradeship are more the rule, just as in civilian life. The modern sailor likes to refer to his vessel as "a happy ship." He may criticize it privately, but in comparison with other battleships of the fleet, his is always the best. To prove it, he will fight for his ship — keep it clean, work hard for accuracy at the guns, and compete enthusiastically in maneuvers, in the ring, on the diamond and gridiron.

High morale is dependent on living, working, and playing in harmony. Because all qualities of Navy men are cultivated, the morale and efficiency of our fleet is not bettered by that of any other in the world.

The Cruisers

Next in importance to battleships in our sea defense are the light and heavy cruisers. The light cruiser, usually of 7,500 tons, carries 6-inch guns. Heavy cruisers, built for speed, carry 8-inch guns. Of modern "underage," or up-to-date, cruisers we have thirty-seven. There will be ninety-one in the two-ocean fleet.

Cruisers are built for speed. Not too much weighed down by heavy armor and guns, they can cut through the water at 35 knots, or about 40 miles per hour. In modern battle the battleship would be protected by an outer line of cruisers, which could maneuver quickly and keep enemy cruisers, destroyers, or submarines busy. Also, the cruiser would be used for scouting and laying smoke screens, or for quick forays to penetrate enemy lines and wreak havoc by gunfire or torpedoes. Scouting planes may be catapulted from its deck to locate the enemy.

The cruiser is the older brother of the battle cruiser, now outmoded. In 1916 we began to build eight battle cruisers of 35,000 tons, but after the Washington Disarmament Conference all but two of these partially built ships were scrapped. The two remaining became our biggest aircraft carriers, the *Lexington* and the *Saratoga*. Since then no more battle cruisers have been built. They are vulnerable because of their lack of armor plate, as was proved recently when the German battleship *Bismarck* blew up the great British battle cruiser with a single shot that penetrated to the *Hood's* magazine. In big ships that cost $75,000,000 or more the United States now relies on the heavier, more ponderous, take-it-best and give-it-best battleship.

Life on a cruiser is like life aboard a battleship, though the two kinds of ships do different jobs in fleet maneuvers. A cruiser is likely to play the part of a lone wolf. For instance, in battle it may be sent out alone to prevent the main line of battleships from being surprised and broken up.

Like the battleship, the cruiser has long been prized and developed as a unit of the fleet. A famous Navy song is "The Armored Cruiser Squadron."

Without Air Power a Modern Fleet Might Quickly Become a Victim of Surprise Attacks by Enemy Warships and Bombers

3 NAVY WINGS

THE UNITED STATES NAVY has been wide-awake in developing an air arm to work in close harmony with the fleet in battle. As early as 1908, officers were sent to learn how to fly with Glenn Curtiss, the famous aircraft inventor, and the flying boat was quickly developed to work with the fleet. Since long-range flying was necessary if aircraft were to be useful to sea forces, Navy pilots became pioneers in long flights. They have held distance records and endured many hardships for the sake of a stronger Navy air force.

The Development of Navy Air Strength

In 1919, the NC-4, under Lieutenant-Commander Read's supervision, was the first airplane to cross the Atlantic. It succeeded in reaching the Azores after the NC-1 and NC-3, its companions, had been forced down on the way. Then it flew on to England. Navy flyers have held the altitude record for planes more than once and have done fine work in many air races. And Admiral Byrd was the first to fly over both the North and South Poles.

Every advance in aircraft development has made the airplane a more important arm of our fleet — an arm ready to support any part of the fleet in any emergency. But the Navy has never organized a separate air corps, because this would make teamwork between aircraft and ships more difficult. The air arm is actually part of the fleet, just as battleships and destroyers are. Some aircraft are stationed ashore for a part of each year, but there are planes always working with the fleet from aircraft carriers, battleships, and cruisers, all of which carry planes of their own.

Today we have in the fleet six aircraft carriers, and twelve more are being built in the Navy's roaring shipyards or planned by naval engineers. On the carriers, squadrons of fighting planes, bombers, torpedo planes, and scout planes vie for higher standards of efficiency. Here rivalry to achieve the best scores in target practices, tactical problems, and record-breaking flying achievements never slackens. New records are constantly being made in getting planes on and off the flight deck, in dive-bombing practice, in scouting maneuvers, and in other jobs that the Navy's air arm must know how to do perfectly.

American naval flyers were the first in the world to perfect dive bombing. Ten years before the Second World War, our pilots knew how to roar down out of the clouds on ships used as targets, sweep the "enemy" decks with machine-gun fire, and drop their bombs with telling accuracy. For many years Navy "flight surgeons" have watched the effects of this type of flying on the men, and new flying techniques have been worked out. As a result, our Navy flyers have no superiors in this most famous kind of aerial warfare.

Airplanes are useful at sea in other ways. They can spot the enemy hundreds of miles away and report his position, course, and speed to the main body of our own fleet. Navy bombers can surprise the enemy by dropping bombs on him from high in the air and our fighters can engage his planes in mortal combat above the clouds. Other planes can fool him by laying smoke screens that blind him, and still others can act as watchdogs along our coasts. Navy airmen can seek out the enemy's "train," or supply ships, and destroy them. By radio they can call our submarines to attack enemy convoys.

The Planes

There are many types of Navy aircraft, and all are necessary to the fleet at sea. The fighting plane (Class VF) is built mainly for speed, agility, and fire power.

25

The job of this small plane is to gain control of the air, if possible, by attacking the enemy — his bombers, scouts, and fighters — with gunfire. It can also swoop down and machine-gun men on the decks of hostile ships or toss light bombs into their midst. Fighting planes, like dive bombers and torpedo and bombing planes, generally operate from carriers, but may be shore-based occasionally.

Torpedo and patrol bombers (Classes VT and VPB) are the largest Navy planes. The torpedo plane can seek out the opposing fleet at anchor, discharge its torpedoes at close range, and play havoc with the big ships before they have an opportunity to get under way, dodge, or send up their own planes. The bomber also is very dangerous to enemy ships and submarines, and to enemy bases as well, since it can carry several thousand pounds of bombs on each trip.

The scout (dive) bomber (Class VSB), carrying fewer bombs than the big bombers, drops its load on the enemy after a nearly vertical dive in which speeds up to five hundred miles per hour are attained. Dive bombers, which are not built for such a long flying range as the big bombers have, would be used in local attacks on the enemy's fleet, to track down and destroy his submarines, and for other similar jobs.

The scouting planes (Class VS) of the Navy have speed, long range, and good defense against their opponents' guns. Their main task is not to attack the enemy but to reconnoiter — to find his ships, to watch the effect on them of our fleet's gunfire, and to radio this information back to our ships. For this work they are equipped with high-powered radio apparatus. Also, because they are in danger of being attacked by enemy fighting planes, they must be fast and have enough machine guns to put up a good fight when cornered. Scouting planes include those used mainly for observation and those used for bombing as well.

Scouting planes operating from battleships and cruisers must be seaplanes, because on those ships there is too little room for running take-offs and landings. The planes are shot into the air by catapults, and on their return are hoisted aboard by a crane.

Additional types of Navy planes are patrol (VP), training (VN), and transport planes (VR and VG). All these are shore-based — that is, they are ordinarily stationed on shore — and do not operate normally with the fleet in battle. Patrol planes, the largest of the fleet, are built for long-range flying and are equipped with radio. Their responsibility is to watch for the enemy and give the alarm to our fleet when necessary. Training planes (VN), as their name indicates, are used for the training of new pilots; they are easy to fly, and are not armed. Amphibian transport planes are big long-range craft that could be used to carry large numbers of men quickly from one part of the fleet to another, or to and from naval bases.

Patrol bombers are, like the patrol planes, big ships with a long range, but they are also equipped to use bombs on the enemy during their patrol missions.

Naval aviation units at sea and ashore are organized into "squadrons" according to their special functions. Thus there are fighting squadrons, patrol squadrons, etc. Each squadron contains about eighteen planes. Squadrons in turn are organized into "wings," each wing consisting of a number of squadrons among which all types of aviation activity are represented.

The Flyers

Most of the Navy's pilots are graduates of Annapolis who have chosen aviation for their career and have been trained at one of the naval air stations, usually Pensacola. Backing up the pilots are thousands of efficient "mechs," or mechanics, and other personnel needed to keep a modern air fleet in smooth working order.

The Navy now is training thousands of officer-aviators at its air stations at Pensacola and Jacksonville, Florida, and Corpus Christi, Texas. These young men are chosen from applicants who are single and are between twenty and twenty-seven,

An Observation Seaplane, One of the "Eyes of the Fleet," Is Catapulted from a Battleship

and have had two years of college or three years in an administrative business position after one year of college. Beginning with preliminary ground-school instruction, they learn to fly training planes and then get practice in advanced flying tactics. After an intensive eight-month course they are full-fledged airmen and are given commissions as ensigns in the Naval Reserve.

The Experts Do Not Sleep

Behind the men who fly the planes and fire the guns is a group of aircraft and gunnery experts who never relax in their efforts to keep the air arm up to date. They make sure that the planes of our Navy are at least as good as, if not better than, any other naval planes in the world.

But this is not their only job. They must also study the effects of flying on the men in the planes, and work out ways of keeping these men at the maximum of physical efficiency while they are in the air. This is called "flight surgery," and our naval experts have been pioneers in it since World War I.

Flight surgery was first thought of during that war, when aviation medical laboratories were established at Mitchell Field, Long Island. Medical officers of the Army and Navy were assigned to this work. Following the war, a whole staff of naval medical officers carried it forward. Only ten per cent of the crashes in World War I were due to defects in planes, and only two per cent were due to enemy marksmanship; but eighty-eight per cent were due to mistakes or defects of the flyers themselves. Since then, long years of study by "flying doctors" have changed these figures; casualties due to the men rather than the planes have been constantly reduced.

Deadly carbon monoxide gas and flights above 15,000 feet without an artificial oxygen supply were two of the worst assassins of airmen. To defeat these assassins, Navy doctors made many experiments. They made power dives with the regular aviators, watching their reactions on the way down and in the pull-outs. They experimented with animals in planes. They would put on fur suits for flights up to 40,000 feet and then would watch pilots' reactions in temperatures of 55 and 60 degrees below zero.

The result is that today planes are so constructed that carbon monoxide does not form in the cockpits and render the pilots unconscious so that they will crash. Men who take planes up to high altitudes are given special equipment to keep them well supplied with life-giving oxygen. Flyers are carefully instructed on how to keep themselves alert and physically fit while in the air. And, from the data assembled by the doctors, various tests have been invented that will show in advance just how fit any naval man is for flying.

WINGS OVER THE SEA

Top Center: A Pair of Fighting Planes. *Upper Left:* A Trio of Scout (Dive) Bombers. *Upper Right:* A Scouting Plane Operating from the Battleship at Lower Right. *Center:* A Patrol Bomber. *Bottom:* A New Long-range Patrol Bomber

Destroyers, Protecting the "Battle Wagons" from the Enemy's Submarines or Launching Their
Own "Fish" at His Capital Ships, Are Always in the Thick of the Fight

Submarines on the Surface Must Be Ever Watchful for Enemy Aircraft

4 SMALLER FIGHTING CRAFT

PROBABLY no ships of the fleet are so attractive to the civilian or the deep-sea sailor as the destroyers. These sea dragons, about three hundred feet long and only ninety feet of beam, are almost all engines. At thirty-five knots, with their heavy corkscrew roll and pitch, they test the stomach and courage of the toughest seadog. In World War I our destroyers aided mightily in convoying two million doughboys to France without the loss of a single man. They were the marvel of all who watched their work in convoying our ships, depth-bombing German submarines, and aiding the mine layers in the northern seas of Europe.

The strongest weapons of the destroyer are its torpedoes, though it carries 5-inch guns and anti-aircraft guns besides. At lightning speed it can dash into the enemy lines by day or night, forcing enemy battleships to change course to escape its deadly torpedo barrage, and thus ruining their marksmanship. It can attack hostile submarines with depth bombs and guns, or it can scout or lay smoke screens to hide our fleet from attackers.

Life aboard is difficult. Naval formalities are not always carried out, but the highest courage and stamina are required to man these little ships in all kinds of weather and to keep them effective in battle.

"Pig Boats"

"Pig boats," as submarines are called by those who man them, are aptly named. The lookout for periscopes at sea is constantly kept in time of war, for nothing can disconcert a man-o'-war so much as an unseen enemy that may suddenly come to the surface right under his nose. As with destroyers, the submarine's best weapon is the torpedo, which may be the scourge of the hostile battleship line and cruiser force alike. Alone, the pig boat is death to enemy commerce and to the line of supply for the main body of an opposing fleet.

The heroism of submarine sailors is familiar to everybody, and Navy men have died, as in the air force, to perfect the modern submersible with its complicated machinery. Diligent research by Navy men themselves has provided means of escape from submarines in trouble, through the Momsen lung and the diving bell.

At New London, Connecticut, is the Navy's submarine school for officers and men. Graduates of the Naval Academy can request submarine duty after two years at sea and after qualifying as watch officers on fighting ships. Knowledge of the pig boats is obtained in courses of three months' duration by officers and men alike. Instruction covers five points: the submarine as a whole, torpedoes, electricity, diesel engineering, and communications. Radio and sound devices are studied; the diesel engine is taken apart, and its mysteries are investigated. Actual operation of submarines at sea forms a large part of the training, and runs are made daily on and under the surface. Student officers and men prepare torpedoes for firing, and these are used in actual firing at targets.

Classes for enlisted men are arranged according to the men's experience at sea, so that they may learn as much as they can and work for higher ratings. There is special instruction in gyrocompass operation, care of storage batteries, and overhaul of diesel engines, torpedoes, and guns. In New London there is a tower 150 feet high in which officers and men learn to "escape" from a submarine by methods worked out experimentally.

Because the pig boat is so complicated, and any error by the crew or defect in construction may mean death to all on board, Navy experts have worked hard to make it safer by engineering research. The loss of a submarine such as that of the *Squalus* or *O-9* does not discourage them, but redoubles their determination to make submarines safer.

"Mosquito Boats"

The Navy is now building fast, and in goodly numbers, the so-called "mosquito boat." This is a torpedo boat about eighty feet long, carrying nine men and equipped with four torpedoes, two machine guns, and a device for laying smoke screens. In war this little craft, which can make up to eighty-five miles an hour, would be a constant threat to any enemy craft. Because it is so small and fast, it might at any moment be able to dash out from behind a smoke screen, launch several torpedoes at an enemy battleship at close range, and skim off again to safety before being hit.

The Train

The "train," or auxiliary vessels of the fleet, are many in number and kinds. The fleet, a sort of floating American city, needs everything that city dwellers need as well as the weapons of war. Oilers, or tankers, have to be always on hand to fill the stomachs of warships and planes with oil and gasoline. Ammunition ships carry powder charges and projectiles and bombs to the big guns and the carriers of the fleet, and are kept busy flying the red powder flag, which is run up when ammuni-

Modern Warships Cannot Operate without Oil, and Tankers Such as This See That They Get It Even When Far from Their Bases

tion is being transferred to another ship. Hospital ships, with doctors and nurses on board to perform major operations and care for the sick, are always ready. Cargo and refrigerator vessels bring up fresh food and supplies.

Of repair ships there are several different kinds: aviation (seaplane) tenders, submarine tenders, and destroyer tenders. With these, practically all repairs can be made at sea, since these floating machine shops are equipped with practically everything that is available in Navy yards.

Transports of all descriptions, sizes, and speeds carry men from one ship and base to another. Some transports must always be ready for the United States Marines, who may be called to action at any moment and must be moved quickly to the scene of trouble.

The Mine Force

The mine force is a distinct part of the battle fleet, and in wartime no other part of the fleet is more exciting. The "layers" and "sweepers" are strange-looking craft of all types. Not built for looks, they do handsome and dangerous deeds. Some are destroyers converted for mine laying.

The "mine host," as this force is called, is a great group of ships that can plant mine fields to protect our coasts, harbors, and naval bases. Once they had laid their thousands of mines in a certain area, it would be very hard indeed for any enemy vessels to get through without being blown up. But this is only one part of the force's job. They may also be called anywhere to carry on the dangerous work of sweeping or blowing up mine fields laid by the enemy, and this is anything but safe. Since warring nations are always developing new kinds of mines, the mine sweepers may be fooled and blown up while they are at work.

A mine sweeper may be a converted trawler, schooner, or yacht. It may look like the second cousin of a thirty-year-old tug. But we can raise our hats to these vessels that "plant, sow, blow up, and scurry away" to a safety that is justly deserved — if they can find it. Enemy mines laid along our coasts would be very dangerous to our fleet and commerce, particularly along our Eastern seaboard, where depths are not so great as in the Pacific and mine fields could be easily anchored.

Many remember that fine summer day in 1918, during the World War I, when the word was flashed that the cruiser *San Diego* had struck a mine and sunk outside New York Harbor. Fortunately, hundreds on board were saved by quick rescue action, since they had time to pull on life preservers and jump overboard into warm summer waters. It is to prevent such disasters in the future — or to cause them to any enemy — that our mine force today continues bravely with its risky work.

34

The Navy's Big Base at Pearl Harbor, Near Honolulu, Hawaiian Islands, Is the "Gibraltar of the Pacific"

5 NAVAL BASES

To DENY a ship a base would be to deny its existence. The closer the fleet to its base of supplies, the more efficient it will be. And the better protected the Navy is by bases of supply far from our shores, the better the chance of keeping America free from invasion. With distant bases, our ships can meet the enemy farther from home.

With its older bases and the newer ones recently acquired from Great Britain in exchange for some of our overage destroyers, our Navy is prepared to keep any hostile navy at a safe distance. In Newfoundland, Bermuda, the Bahamas, Antigua, St. Lucia, Trinidad, Greenland, and British Guiana we are building air bases to give us control of waters hundreds of miles from our Eastern seaboard. Patrol planes can radio to the United States Fleet the approach of an enemy long before he reaches mid-ocean. Likewise in the Pacific the Navy has bases on Kodiak, Midway, Palmyra, and Johnston Islands, and in Alaska. Our base at Pearl Harbor, Hawaii, is the most powerful of all — the "Gibraltar of the Pacific."

Our ring of island bases extends all around the United States from the Aleutian Islands off Alaska to Panama, and up the East Coast to the Arctic Circle, so that the eyes of the fleet will ever be on all approaches to the American mainland. In addition we have naval air bases along our East and West Coasts — twenty-six of them. All are or will be equipped to train airmen and overhaul aircraft, and will be used for lookout stations to protect our long seacoasts.

Land bases for the fleet are strategically located around the United States. We have Navy Yards at Boston, New York, Philadelphia, Washington, Norfolk, Portsmouth, Mare Island in California, Charleston, and New Orleans. The base at Panama is heavily protected by our island strongholds to the east and west and by its own anti-aircraft and submarine bases at Coco Solo in the Canal Zone. On the West Coast the fleet can be based at San Diego, San Pedro, or Mare Island, or at Bremerton, in Washington.

Fleet bases receive a careful consideration from our naval strategists. They are carefully chosen and heavily defended. A good example is Chesapeake Bay, with its entrances netted at Capes Henry and Charles, and with its wide sea spaces, where hundreds of ships can be anchored in calm, protected waters.

The ideal base should be accessible to the sea and have natural protection and plenty of room for maneuvering. Thus Puget Sound, with its long entrance from the straits that guard it, culminating in the deep waters of Seattle and Bremerton, becomes a safe haven. Hawaii, not so well protected by nature, is nevertheless more suitable, since Pearl Harbor with its wide waters is easily accessible.

Naval tacticians must always think of the convenience of bases. During naval warfare not only would our ships need quantities of supplies in a hurry, but ships damaged by the enemy would need near-by bases to which they could limp for quick repairs. At the base the hurt ship would have instant attention from highly skilled mechanics and Navy Yard workmen. The quicker she could be repaired, the sooner she could speed back to strengthen the battle line.

In any naval war our Navy's commanders, while keeping near our bases, would try to lure the enemy away from his bases. Then his long line of supplies could be cut and his damaged ships finished off, perhaps, before they could get back home.

Besides its major Navy Yards, the Navy has equipped supply depots that can take the load off the Navy Yards as far as food and other staple needs are concerned.

The fate of the Spanish fleet when it met the Americans at Santiago in the Spanish-American War, and the defeat of the Russian fleet by the Japanese at Tsu-Shima in 1906, prove that a navy is only as strong as its bases. The United States Navy intends to keep its bases strong and add to their ever-growing numbers.

36

Some Navy Uniforms — Enlisted Men (left): Dungarees; Full Dress Whites; Dress Blues. Officers (right): White Service Dress; Blue Service Dress; Full Dress

6 A SHIP'S ORGANIZATION

A MODERN WARSHIP is the very last thing that could "run itself." Even in the excitement of battle practice, when everything on board might look like confusion to a landlubber, every officer and man is doing a specially assigned job.

The Officers

The top man on a naval vessel, the captain, is virtually a "king." To officers and men he is the "skipper," or "old man." Every activity is under his supervision. Often he is a lonely man, because he lives mostly by himself, according to Navy custom. On battleships the captain, corresponding to an Army colonel, is a four-striper. His chief assistant is the executive officer, a three-striper, or commander, ranking with a lieutenant colonel in the Marines or Army. The executive officer is in charge of all ship activities, reporting only to the captain and carrying out his orders. He sits at the head of the senior officers' mess, with other officers grouped about him according to rank. The ship's departments are headed usually by lieutenant commanders, who rank with Army majors.

The ordnance (gunnery) officer sees to the upkeep of guns and training of gun crews. He sees that ammunition and powder are on hand. Under him are turret officers, usually lieutenants senior grade, corresponding to Army captains. They are responsible for turret efficiency and the training of turret crews, which are marked off into divisions 1, 2, 3, etc. Broadside gun divisions may have lieutenants or lieutenants junior grade in charge. (Junior grade lieutenants correspond to Army first lieutenants.) Also responsible to the gunnery officer, on ships that carry torpedoes, is the torpedo officer. Officers in charge of divisions of anti-aircraft guns also report to the gunnery officer.

The ship's navigator heads his own department, and on battleships he generally is a lieutenant commander. He is in charge of navigating instruments, charts, and compasses. He supervises quartermasters and signalmen, and is responsible to the captain for ascertaining the ship's position by true sights and by dead reckoning.

The engineering officer, a lieutenant commander, is responsible for the ship's engines. The first lieutenant is in charge of ship maintenance and upkeep. Thus, if the side has to be cleaned of barnacles in port, or if double bottoms must be chipped and painted, he sees that this is done. He is also damage-control officer.

The supply corps officer gets all necessary food, clothing, and general stores for the ship's company. The medical officer supervises the ship's hospital and guards the health of the crew. The ship's dental officer, who attends to seagoing toothaches, is junior to the medical officer. Every major ship has also its own chaplain, who conducts religious services, supervises the library, and does welfare work.

Warrant officers are enlisted men who, through years of experience, have gained "warrant rank" after being chief petty officers. They are practical experts in engineering, gunnery, and electricity.

The first lieutenant's department and each division officer for turrets, guns, and engineering have junior officers for assistants. They are ensigns or junior-grade lieutenants and have their own junior officers' mess.

The Enlisted Men

Chief petty officers, or "C.P.O.'s," are often called the backbone of the Navy. They have worked up to the highest rank below that of commissioned and warrant officers, and have their own mess. Each division has its C.P.O., who is the direct tie between its officers and enlisted men. C.P.O.'s often have from twelve to sixteen years' experience in the Navy. Among them are chief radiomen, chief torpedomen, gunners' mates, electricians, signalmen, quartermasters, water tenders, and boatswain's mates. They become experts through long association with the ship to

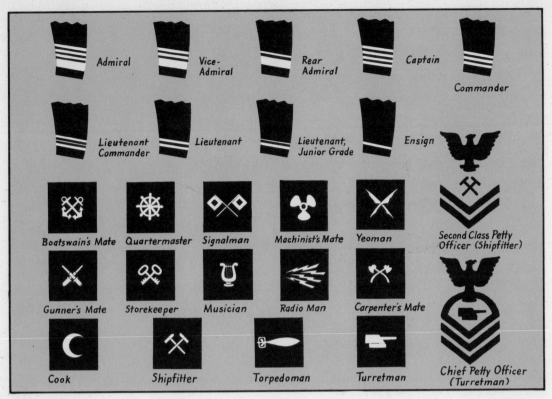

These Are Some of the Insignia Worn in the Navy. Those in the Two Top Rows Indicate Officers' Ranks. Those in the Three Bottom Rows Indicate Branches of Service of Enlisted men; Their Use in Petty Officers' Insignia Is Shown at the Right.

which they are attached. Under them come enlisted men's ratings, such as quartermaster first and second class down to the seaman first and second class and ordinary seaman.

Ship Organization on Smaller Units

Organization on cruisers, destroyers, aircraft carriers, and submarines resembles the set-up on the battleship. Except on cruisers and aircraft carriers, the rank of the commanding officer is lower, with corresponding lower ranks filling positions junior to the captain. A cruiser will have a junior captain in command — that is, a captain with less years of service than a battleship's captain. The executive officer will be a commander relatively junior, in years of service, to a battleship's executive officer. A destroyer leading a group of destroyers is under the control of a commander acting as captain, but other destroyers in the group are usually commanded by lieutenant commanders. Lieutenants and lieutenant commanders are the top officers on submarines. In the air force, commanders are usually in charge of squadrons, with captains and even rear admirals commanding patrol wings. Ships of the train force are officered according to the size and importance of the ships.

A Battleship's Deck Is One of the Cleanest Places on Earth

7 THE NAVY LIFE

PRACTICALLY every man in the Navy, whether officer or enlisted man, works hard — and likes it. Navy life is not all thrilling adventure, or seeing the world through a porthole, or firing guns. The pay does not make the men rich, and there are times when a man wishes he were home instead of far away at sea. But Navy men say there is something in the career that makes up for these things. Interesting jobs, comradeship, rugged health, recreations, enthusiastic patriotism — these are the reasons why men join the Navy and stay with it.

The Commissioned Officers

Commissioned officers, as distinguished from enlisted men, occupy a preferred position. They receive higher pay, have their own staterooms and mess aboard ship, are addressed as "Sir" by the men, and don't have to do such jobs as swabbing decks and oiling engines. Since their pay is higher, it is often possible for their families to move from port to port to be on hand when father's ship comes in. Most regular

Scout Bombers Maneuver over Cruisers and a "Mosquito Boat"

officers are graduates of Annapolis, though many have worked up from the ranks.

Every officer has worked hard for his position; it has not been handed to him on a silver platter. As a midshipman at Annapolis he has to study night and day for four years, and during summer cruises on warships he has his taste of all the jobs that sailors have to do. Even after graduation, he is expected to continue studying and never relax in his efforts to become a better officer. As a leader of men ashore and afloat, he carries heavy responsibilities, because the lives of men and the safety of Navy property often depend upon his quick decisions. He must be ready for all emergencies — the crash of a plane, the handling of a damaged ship, sailors in trouble, and a hundred and one other situations that demand a cool head and a loyal heart. Most of all he must be a friend to his men — an officer whom they will respect and whose orders they will instantly carry out, but also one who they know will give them a square deal and stand by them whatever happens.

The Enlisted Men

Below the lowest rank of commissioned officer, that of ensign, are the vast numbers of enlisted men who, under officers' orders, do the actual work of running ships, firing guns, keeping planes in good condition, and maintaining Navy property. These men, although leading a life separate from that of commissioned officers ashore and afloat, know their importance to the Navy and have a strong *esprit de corps*.

To get into the Navy, the applicant must pass a rigid physical examination. He may be as young as sixteen or as old as thirty-three. Usually he is a high-school graduate, or has had at least two years of high-school education. A few recruits hold college degrees.

Enlistment in the Navy is for six years. The recruit is first given eight weeks of training at one of the Navy's training stations — at Newport, the Great Lakes, Norfolk, or San Diego. Here he learns the routine he may expect aboard ship and goes through a steady course of daily drills with weapons and boats. He learns to tie knots and splice ropes, to box the compass, to swim, to signal with semaphore and signal flags, to respect his chief petty officer and the other officers who are preparing him for life afloat. Once aboard ship, he must know how to lash and air a hammock, to keep a full bag neat and clean and ready for inspection, and to meet the day's work with a grin and the will to learn, so that he may attain promotion as rapidly as possible.

The enlisted man of our Navy is the finest type of American youth. He is clean, responsible, ready for work and play alike. The days of the old roughhousing sailor men are gone, for the modern American bluejacket, like his brother in industry, is a sober citizen.

The sailor, as a rule, saves his money, although on occasion he throws it away. He is happy-go-lucky, and yet he is serious. Naturally he enjoys the company of the best-looking girl he can find. But on the whole he is a lonesome fellow, for usually he comes into a strange city and knows no one. He does not particularly enjoy wandering the streets, but what else can he do? He would like to come more often into people's homes, but the people he sees are usually strangers and pass him by.

Citizens ashore who are aware of the importance and value of the American sailor support his Y.M.C.A.'s and recreation centers. Dances and dinners are sometimes arranged for him, and he is very appreciative of such favors. These are good investments, too, for the American bluejacket is working for every American citizen; he is our man, our first line of defense.

Navy Pocketbooks

The Navy is no place for making mints of money. It offers no more than a bare living to all. It does, however, offer security to the men and their families.

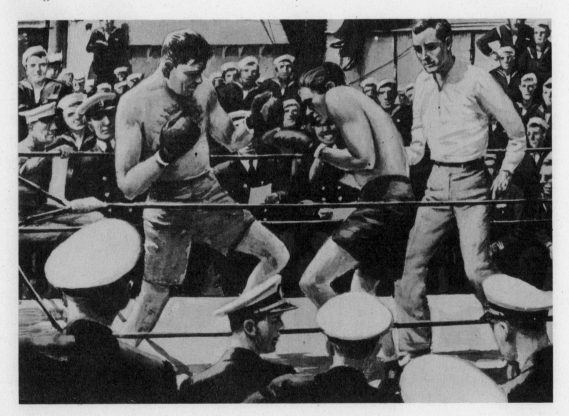

The Navy Supplies Its Own Entertainment on Shipboard

Consider the pay of the captain of a battleship, keeping in mind the number of men he commands and the value of his $100,000,000 "business," in comparison with the pay of equally high executives in civilian life. One can hardly say that the naval officer works for money. The Navy, like medicine and other scientific careers, is a profession. It involves being away from home at Christmas time, leaving one's family at critical periods in home life, and never counting on being in a certain place tomorrow — for the naval show *must* go on.

To compensate for his thin pocketbook, the Navy man may retire after thirty or forty years of service, with enough to live on "uncomfortably," as those with less frugal tastes would testify.

The midshipman at Annapolis is paid $780 a year for going to school, and this amount is sufficient for him to meet the current expenses of living at the Naval Academy. Out of this he pays for his uniforms, mess, books, and all things concerned with the business of life, such as laundry, soap, and tooth paste. Each year he tries to save something so that when he gets a month's leave he will have a little to spend while he is away from the Academy. This is possible because he never sees

On a Man-of-War the Use of Hammocks Saves Valuable Space, but on Many Ships the Sailors Now Enjoy Folding Bunks

44

his salary during the school year, and the amount allowed in his pockets by regulation is but a few dollars. Upon graduation he has officer's uniforms to buy, and from his ensign's pay he must foot his share of the mess bill aboard ship. As a famous admiral once said in addressing an Annapolis graduating class: "You now inherit a commission in the Navy and join that singular group who have gone before you in trying to meet each month's bills."

The pay of an ensign is $1,500 a year, and of a junior lieutenant $2,100, to which are added allowances of 5 per cent for each three-year period of service. Added to this is a rental and subsistence allowance. Officers in the flying service receive 50 per cent more than their base pay, because their work is more dangerous, and "submariners" get 25 per cent extra. The maximum that any officer of the rank of captain or lower can earn is $6,000 yearly in base pay, to which rental and subsistence allowances are added.

Enlisted men in the Navy are provided with their first outfits and their meals and lodging, and begin at $21 per month while in their training station. After four months' service, they get $30 per month, and on becoming second-class seamen they receive $36 per month. They pay for their uniforms, however, after getting their first outfit. A first-class seaman receives $54 a month, and a chief petty officer with a permanent standing, $126 a month.

There are other emoluments, too. Upon completion of four years' service, the enlisted man gets a 10 per cent raise in base pay. Thereafter he gets increases of 5 per cent up to 25 per cent for each four years' service. Those in submarine service draw extra pay of from $5 to $30 per month.

Officers who have been retired for physical reasons get for the rest of their lives 75 per cent of the base pay they were getting when they were retired. If retired for other reasons, such as length of service, they receive 2½ per cent per year of service in the rank in which they are retired.

There is no regular retired pay for enlisted men, unless they have served thirty years, but they may be pensioned for injuries sustained in line of duty. Also, after sixteen and twenty years' service they may be placed in the Fleet Reserve, where they will always be on call and draw from 58½ per cent to 75 per cent of the pay they would normally receive on active duty. Pensions for men retired because of injuries suffered in service may be as high as 75 per cent of their pay, and may range up to $187.50 a month in cases of total disability.

Promotions of Officers

Since 1916, naval officers have been promoted by selection. This became necessary because promotion was slow and it was desirable to hold out the chance of advancement to unusually able men. Selection boards which choose officers to be promoted consist of seven officers, all senior to the rank for which the candidate is being considered.

No officer looks with glee upon the opportunity to sit on a selection board. Often the board must choose for promotion only one of two officers whose records are equally good. Upon human judgment rests the responsibility of making one man's career and spoiling another's. To be "passed over" is a fear that enters every officer's heart when "his number is up." The system, though still imperfect, is the best that has been evolved for promotions up to captain or rear admiral.

The true naval officer is philosophical about promotion. He knows that a minor misdemeanor in his record may work against him. He looks upon a fellow officer who has been passed over with a good deal of sympathy, knowing that it might have been himself. It has been argued that favoritism plays its part in the selection system; but, as five of seven officers must pass on a fellow officer's fitness, such criticism is hardly justified. The Navy does its best.

Navy Men Ashore

It has long been a Navy custom to shift line officers to different jobs so that they may become thoroughly familiar with all branches of naval activity. To "fight a fleet," which is the ultimate goal in the life of all admirals, these higher officers must know every assignment in the Navy and must have participated in as many of them as possible during their careers. All officers jealously guard their own "fitness" reports, so that when they come up for selection and promotion they will have served in the right positions in accordance with their ranks. You will often hear an officer say, "I haven't had enough battleship duty," or "Perhaps I stayed too long in submarines," or "John Doe was passed over — he remained too long on the staffs of three admirals."

After graduating from Annapolis, an officer normally remains at sea for six years. Then he has his first shore duty, which may last two years, or even three if it is felt that he cannot be spared. But most naval officers ashore always look forward to their next duty afloat.

Officers on shore duty may be sent to advanced schools in strategy, ordnance, and engineering, such as those mentioned earlier in this chapter. They also may act as executives in Navy Yards, where they superintend shipbuilding, as industrial managers in naval factories, or as members of the large naval communication system which spans the world. Many of them are pilots of the air force, assigned to train

new pilots at the air stations and to practice overland flying, dogfighting, dive bombing, and other tasks that they might have to undertake in time of war.

Enlisted men also are trained ashore. They may attend the submarine school in New London, Connecticut, or be assigned to duty in Navy Yards, at the Naval Academy, or at air bases. Many of them are instructors at training schools, teaching new recruits the ways of the sea. Others are attached to air stations where, although they may not be among the pilots, they fill many necessary and exciting aviation jobs. Still others fill the Navy's needs for pharmacists, painters, mechanics, cooks, and other skilled workers ashore. Many of them have had the opportunity to learn their trades since their enlistment.

Only the Finest Become Commissioned Officers and Win Promotions

Unceasing Study of Naval Tactics at the War College Helps to Make Good Officers

8 THE MAKING OF OFFICERS

OUR NAVY is so vast and complicated, and its responsibility is so great, that the officers who give the orders must be chosen from among the best manhood of America and must be given long years of highly technical education and practice. Without intelligent and experienced officers, the most powerful warships would be useless in the defense of our country. From the Chief of Naval Operations in Washington down to the ensigns and warrant officers, every officer must be capable of filling his job in any emergency.

The Naval Academy

Most of our Navy's officers have had their basic naval education at the United States Naval Academy at Annapolis, Maryland. After four years of intensive technical and physical education at the Academy, which ranks with the best engineering institutions in the nation, the young graduates go out to the fleet as ensigns or into the Marines as second lieutenants, and there begin their real careers.

Young men who aspire to a naval officer's career may be admitted to the Academy after getting an appointment from their local Congressman and then passing stiff physical and mental entrance examinations. Each Congressman is now allowed five such appointments, which are usually given to winners of competitive examinations, and the largest classes in the Academy's history are now in prospect. Each year one hundred extra appointments to Annapolis are given to enlisted men of the Navy who can qualify by passing the rigid entrance tests, and one hundred more go to the Naval Reserve enlisted forces.

To midshipmen, Annapolis is known as "Crabtown-on-the-Bay," and here a lingo has developed that has come to be known by seafaring men as "the language." A floor is a "deck"; a "drag" is a midshipman's girl friend; a "yard engine" is the daughter of an officer living inside the grounds. A freshman is a "plebe," and a sophomore a "youngster." To "frap the pap" is to be put on the report for failing in one's duties, the Spanish language department is "dago," and so on. With these terms is mixed the slang of the sea.

The course at Annapolis is ordinarily four years long, but in times when war has been threatened it has been limited to three or three and a half years.

Every day of the midshipman's life is arduous. He answers the bugle at six in the morning, and is ready for quarters (the call to his station) twenty minutes later. Throughout the morning and afternoon, his hours are filled with instruction and study of the hardest courses known to men. By the time he has reached his first-class (senior) year, the midshipman himself marvels at his ability to soak up knowledge

Midshipmen at Annapolis, in Training to Become Officers of the Fleet, Rival the West Pointers in the Perfection of Their Drilling

in navigation, seamanship, ordnance and gunnery, steam and electrical engineering. and all of the higher mathematics. He watches his marks carefully, because he "hits the tree" (is in danger of flunking out) if he falls below a "2.5," which is passing (a "4.0" being perfect). Normally, two thirds of the young men entering the Naval Academy weather the course and, at the end of the four years, see the day when they can throw their caps in the air and sing "No More Rivers to Cross."

But there are more rivers — and some oceans. Upon graduation, the young ensign is only beginning a long career which may end by his becoming Commander-in-Chief of the United States Fleet. Whether or not he goes that high in rank, his education is never finished. On shipboard and on land he must be constantly acquiring new information in order to be a good officer. Many Annapolis graduates attend the submarine school at New London, the postgraduate school at Annapolis for advanced training in professional subjects, or the Massachusetts Institute of Technology, Columbia, Michigan, California Tech, and other universities where they can become experts in technical subjects. Other officers are sent to the Naval War College.

The Naval War College

One of the chief centers of naval brainwork in the world is the War College at Newport, Rhode Island. To the War College go many naval officers to learn the science of war at sea. Some courses at the War College last a year, and a regular correspondence course is offered to officers of the fleet who are not free to be in Newport. Expert civilian lecturers supplement the instruction given by naval officers of the highest experience and training in their profession.

The War College is essentially for line officers (officers of the battle fleet), but staff officers — that is, medical, supply, and engineering officers — are found in its student body more and more. Officers of the United States Marines also take advanced courses, and some Army officers come to this fountain of knowledge just as some Naval officers attend the Army's General Staff School and the Army Industrial College.

At the War College battles are fought, war games are carried out in miniature, and enemies are sunk, while on occasion a particularly accomplished officer may take the "enemy" fleet into battle and sink our own Navy. If American naval officers could be sold to the highest bidder, many of them would probably bring "top prices" from some of the other navies of the world!

Reserve Officers

Ordinarily the Naval Academy supplies the fleet with all or most of the officers it needs. But in times of national danger the Navy must be able to get officers faster than the Academy can produce them with its four-year course. To man the two-ocean Navy now being built, with its 925 ships and 15,000 planes, 33,500 officers as well as 461,000 men will be needed. For some time, therefore, the Navy has maintained a Naval Reserve Officers' Training Corps, with branches at many universities all over the country. In addition, 5,000 reserve ensigns have been trained at sea and in various shore schools selected by the Navy. Still another source of officers are the engineering colleges, many graduates of which are now joining the Navy as officers and thus contributing their technical education to the national defense.

One of the largest programs for the training of officers was worked out quickly when it was decided recently to create the 5,000 reserve ensigns already mentioned. In a few weeks, these young men were recruited as reserve midshipmen. They were then sent to sea on battleships for thirty days, and after that were given a three-month course at the Naval Academy, Northwestern University, or on board the Receiving Ship at New York City. Thousands of our best American youths responded; the lists were soon filled from college men anxious to go to sea. On graduation, they join the fleet as ensigns in the U. S. Naval Reserve.

Thousands of Young Americans Become Reserve Officer-aviators at the Naval Air Stations

A Marine Landing Party Takes Part in Hemisphere Defense Maneuvers

9 THE MARINES AND THE COAST GUARD

THE MARINE CORPS is an honored part of the Navy. Some landlubbers believe marines and sailors are in constant argument, but nothing can be further from the truth. They know they are necessary to one another. At sea they work hand in hand to make the Navy efficient. On shore they are often seen on liberty together. In battle they help each other at the guns and in landing-force operations.

There was a time in our history when we did not have a Navy, but we have always had a Marine Corps. It was organized in 1775. Since then, "The Soldiers of the Sea" have always proved themselves brave men, and protectors of American interests all over the world. Yesterday we heard of them in Nicaragua and Haiti; today they are in China; tomorrow they will be wherever their country calls them. In World War I

52

they fought in France with distinction, and if our country is again forced into war they can be counted upon to fight with equal distinction. Their motto is *Semper Fidelis,* "ever loyal."

Head of the Marine Corps is the Major General Commandant, who works with the Chief of Naval Operations. The Marines have their own bases as well as training stations, and Quantico (Virginia), Parris Island (South Carolina), and San Diego (California) are the homes of their major divisions. Once a year they voyage with the fleet to southern waters and there, in maneuvers, practice landings on "hostile" territory with rifles, machine guns, field pieces, and other weapons.

Marines have their own aircraft and flyers, and their own Basic School at Philadelphia for training young officers in duties at sea, in the field, and in garrisons. The United States Marine Band, like the Navy Band that plays for the midshipmen at Annapolis, has become internationally famous.

The strength of the Corps varies from 17,000 to 75,000 officers and men. Because the Corps is small in numbers, it has been able to maintain the highest tradition.

The Fleet Marine Force consists of infantry, artillery, tanks, signal corps, engineering and chemical troops, and an air force. Marines on battleships man units of broadside batteries, police their own part of the ship, function in ship ceremonies, and help regular Navy men in taking watches.

Most Marine officers are graduates of the Naval Academy, West Point, and civilian colleges. (Twenty-five come from each class at Annapolis.) Some have risen from the ranks, having shown their ability and passed stiff examinations.

Marine officers, like naval officers, never find their educations completed. As second lieutenants they attend the Basic School, and as more mature officers they attend an advanced school in strategy and tactics at Quantico. They study at the Army and Navy War Colleges and the Army Command General Staff School.

Ranks correspond to those in the Army, the lowest commissioned officer being second lieutenant, and the highest, major general.

The Marine Corps Reserve is organized like the Naval Reserve. The Fleet Reserve contains infantry battalions, aviation squadrons, and an artillery battalion. Some college students enlist in the Marine Corps Volunteer Reserve during their sophomore year, and take rigid field training during summer vacations. Upon graduation from college and after completing twelve weeks of intensive training, they are commissioned second lieutenants in the Reserve.

The Coast Guard

For over a hundred years the Coast Guard has patterned its organization and

Marine Parachute Troops Practice Surprise Attacks

administration on those of the Navy. Under existing law the Coast Guard operates under the Treasury Department in time of peace and as part of the Navy in time of war. Its training and traditions are therefore closely allied to naval operations. The magnificent work of the Coast Guard is well known, and constantly brings forth the admiration of the people of the United States for its thrilling rescues of sailing men without distinction as to flag, nationality, or race. Founded in 1790, before a Navy Department existed, it has always lived up to its motto, *Semper Paratus*, "always prepared." The Coast Guard tradition is built on the double duty of defending our shores in time of war and serving humanity in time of peace.

Officers of the Coast Guard are trained at its own academy in New London, Connecticut. Here a course not unlike that of the Naval Academy prepares young men to handle any emergency they may meet at sea. Cadet cruises of three months' duration under sail and steam give the trainee practical training in seamanship, navigation, gunnery, and ship handling.

All are familiar with the life-saving stations along our coasts, operated and controlled as part of the Coast Guard service. Each station is a complete unit, with boats, apparatus, and equipment for the saving of life at sea.

In World War I, the Coast Guard cutters served with distinction as part of the Navy in convoying our troops and supplies to Europe. In the Gibraltar area, one of the most dangerous in the war zone, ships of the Coast Guard daily protected cargoes of the Allies.

Because the North Atlantic sea lanes are constantly menaced by icebergs, the International Ice Patrol was organized. Coast Guard ships now help to protect millions of lives and billions in shipping in those waters.

During the development of Alaska after its purchase by the United States from Russia, the Coast Guard began laying out channels for commerce, catching smugglers, and locating sites for customs houses. Locating fishing banks and coaling stations for merchant ships was part of this work. The Coast Guard also supervises the fishing and fur industries in northern waters.

Coast Guard cutters, normally of 2,000 tons, are designed for heavy work rather than great speed. Following World War I, many naval destroyers were turned over to Coast Guard units that required speedy vessels. All manner of craft, large and small, now make up the patrols.

Other Coast Guard duties are carried out by shore units trained in radio and intelligence work. These units are valuable adjuncts to the Federal Bureau of Investigation and Naval Intelligence.

The officers and men of the Navy are strong in their praise of the Coast Guard, and between the two services there exists a bond of loyalty and devotion to duty. In time of emergency the Navy knows that its sister service can be called upon for all manner of sacrifice and can carry out any mission, however dangerous.

Coast Guard Cutters, Meeting Emergencies at Sea and along Our Coasts in Time of Peace, Join the Navy in Time of War

55

The Navy Department Is the Brain of the Fleet

10 THE NAVY DEPARTMENT

THE HEADQUARTERS of our seagoing forces is the Navy Department at Washington. Here naval policy is worked out according to the policy of our government, and from here the admirals of the fleet and the commanders of naval stations get orders.

The High Command

Heading the Department is the Secretary of the Navy, who with his assistants is appointed by the President. Civilians are appointed so that the Navy will always be under direct representatives of the people of the United States.

Next to the Secretary is the Chief of Naval Operations, likewise appointed by the President. The highest-ranking officer of the Navy, he corresponds to the Chief of Staff of the Army. He works directly under the Secretary, and the operation of the fleet is his responsibility. The War Plans Division, Naval Communications, Coast Guard vessels in time of war, ship movements, Naval Intelligence, naval districts,

56

and fleet training are all under his watchful eye. He also consults with the General Board, a group of the highest-ranking naval officers who help to work out Navy policies and to decide on the ships and planes the Navy needs.

With the Secretary, he confers with the President, who is Commander-in-Chief of the Army and Navy.

Heading the various divisions under the Chief are rear admirals on shore duty — men of the highest experience in their profession.

Naval Intelligence

A very important division of the Navy Department is that of Naval Intelligence. Its job is to collect and distribute information of value to the Navy. It keeps naval records and maintains naval attachés in embassies abroad. It also works with investigating services of other government departments, such as the Federal Bureau of Investigation, to protect Navy property and secrets, as well as factories producing Navy equipment.

The Bureau of Navigation and Other Bureaus

Following are the various Navy bureaus and their responsibilities:

Bureau of Navigation: Procurement, education, training, discipline, and assignments of officers and men of the Navy, including the Naval Reserve and Reserve Officers' Training Corps.

Bureau of Ships: Building and maintenance of ships.

Bureau of Ordnance: Arming of Navy ships and shore establishments.

Bureau of Aeronautics: Aircraft research; equips Navy with its air forces.

Bureau of Yards and Docks: Public works of the Navy, such as buildings, dry docks, naval-base construction projects, and heating, lighting, and even telephone systems.

Bureau of Supplies and Accounts: Purchasing fuel, food, clothing, etc. (Among its workers are the "paymasters" of the Navy, who, on the first and fifteenth of every month, become very popular with officers and men.)

Bureau of Medicine and Surgery: Naval hospitals; procurement of doctors; medical care at stations and on ships.

The Navy maintains also its own legal department, under the office of the Judge Advocate General. His assistants are regular naval officers who have been legally trained to work out legal problems for the Navy.

Navy Buying

The Joint Army and Navy Munitions Board makes it possible for the Army and

Submarines, the "Scourge of the Seas," Maneuver with the Fleet While Patrol Planes Fly Overhead

the Navy to do much of their buying together. On this Board are Army and Navy officers, and they often come together to discuss problems common to both services. If both branches wish to get training planes, for instance, joint orders may be placed by one service or the other, with the two aviation branches working in harmony. The Army may buy the planes, the Navy may obtain the engines for both, and by thus pooling their needs the services may save the taxpayers millions of dollars. If the Navy needed mules, it would undoubtedly leave the buying of them to the Army, and if the Army needed goats, as it did on one experimental occasion, the Navy could probably be of real help through its familiarity with the strength and peculiar habits of that animal. The goat, you will remember, is the mascot of the Naval Academy.

Navy Research

The Navy must always be alert to adopt and develop useful inventions. Each year thousands of devices are submitted to the Navy Department, and, though many are useless, there are always some that may help to close a watertight door more easily, raise a submarine, elevate a gun, stop a leak, or do something else that the Navy wants done well. All new devices or suggestions are examined carefully and are discarded only if they are obviously worthless.

From naval officers themselves, familiar through long experience at sea with what is needed, come many of the best ideas. Some ideas are not conceived overnight but remain experimental for years, until long hours of work and many minds have perfected them.

You will remember how Commanders Momsen and McCann worked for years to perfect their submarine escape devices, and how Navy doctors studied the reactions of pilots of aircraft. Similar effort has gone into experimental work on ships. Among recent developments are new types of gyrocompasses, anti-rolling devices for ships for use in heavy weather, and many types of fire-control instruments.

There are always new devices in engineering to be tried out and high-pressure boilers to be experimented with. The Navy maintains many experimental laboratories and also a ship-model basin, where the behavior of miniature vessels under all conditions can be measured in terms of combatant ship sizes. The Navy has an experimental engineering station at Annapolis, an experimental boiler station in Philadelphia, and, also in Philadelphia, an aircraft factory where new models and devices are tried out in actual practice. Experiments with powder, shells, bombs, mines, and small-arm ammunition are constantly going on. The naval gun factory at Washington, D. C., is one of the most interesting of the places where the Navy is keeping abreast of the latest and best methods for its ships, engines, and guns.

Radio Is a Vital Part of the Navy's "Nervous System"

11 NAVAL COMMUNICATIONS AND NAVIGATION

FASCINATING is the vast, complicated communications system of the Navy. It is as necessary for naval units to keep in touch with each other as it is for them to have compasses and maps so they will know where they are going. Navy technicians take every advantage of modern science in devising methods of communication. If the Navy Department is the "brain" of the Navy, communications is its "nervous system."

Electrical Messengers

When wireless was in its cradle, the Navy was quick to see its possibilities. When Marconi's invention was announced, naval officers were immediately assigned to work with the inventor. Since then the Navy has kept up with all radio developments. Radio has become a part of the course of every midshipman at Annapolis, and many enlisted men have received like training.

During World War I, the Navy trained 10,000 wireless operators at the Harvard Radio School, and the United States was dotted with naval sending and receiving stations. Today, Navy Radio sets aside days to talk with amateur operators on the air waves, and is in touch with thousands of radio enthusiasts, many of whom become members of the Naval Reserve communications service.

The Navy's laboratories buzz with the activity of technicians developing new ways to use radio. Since the Navy must keep abreast with or ahead of foreign navies, in the use of this magic messenger, no possibility of improving its efficiency is overlooked. The naval experts consult frequently with radio experts outside, and investigate all incoming suggestions of possible value.

One of the problems of the communications experts is that of devising and keeping secret the naval codes. Much information passed between naval units is not secret, and it does not matter if it is overheard. But some of it the Navy prefers to keep from falling into the hands of persons who might misuse it. In wartime, especially, it would be vital to keep the enemy from learning the intentions and movements of our forces. Hence the Navy is constantly developing new codes, since it is

The Effectiveness of Each Unit of the Fleet — and of the Whole Fleet — Depends upon Fleet Communications

assumed that one which has been in use for some time has been worked out by unfriendly listeners. The men who work on the codes have an endless job — a job full of brain-wracking mathematics mixed with guesswork and ingenuity — but their work is indispensable and as "detectives" in their line they have few equals.

The Navy does not rely entirely on its own radio system. It co-operates with the commercial radio companies, and the telephone, telegraph, and cable companies, which cover the earth.

Signaling

Radio is the Navy's main way of sending messages, but older methods are still useful. Visual signaling at sea at night is done with searchlights fitted with shutters and strong lamps to send the dot-and-dash code. By day, signalmen and quarter-masters use flaghoists and flag codes, the letters being varicolored, and diagrammed flags and pennants. In signaling with flags, positions of flags denote letters. These are international codes, and are the means of communication between ships of all nations.

Navigation is as old as mankind, though as recently as the days of Columbus the mariner often did not know where he was going, or where he was after he got there, and doubted very much whether he'd ever get home. Navigators today, with charts of the seven seas, sextants with which they "shoot" the sun and stars, and with knowledge of tides, currents, wind, and sea, can tell at any moment just about where their ship is. To the landlubber it seems miraculous when the navigator says, "We'll pick up Long Island Lightship at 8:07," or "Today we'll cross the Equator about noon."

The Naval Observatory at Washington aids navigators by broadcasting time signals many times daily, and is the official check on Standard Time in the United States and its possessions. At sea, navigators can correct chronometers by these signals, which are used on shore by scientists whose timing must be split-second. Time signals are sent round the world by rebroadcasts from radio and telegraph companies.

The Naval Observatory, "in constant touch" also with stars and planets, collects data for the *Nautical Almanac,* the Navigator's "Bible." Solar and lunar eclipses are among the main subjects of interest. Another responsibility of the Observatory is the repair and conditioning of nautical and aerological instruments — a service essential to the Navy.

The Hydrographic Office

Charts of the seas and harbors are prepared for the navigator by the Navy Hydrographic Office. The Navy and merchant marine, as well as private yachtsmen, can get charts for all the world for the price of printing and paper. Aviation charts are also part of the Office's output.

The Hydrographic Office's research in oceanography is of constant help to the mariner. Some 300,000 soundings have been taken by naval ships in the past few years, and naval charts are constantly kept up to date to follow the shifting seas and their perils to navigators. The *U. S. S. Bushnell*, operating in the Pacific in 1930-1940, covered 76,000 nautical square miles, surveying island shoals for sea and air transportation facilities. The *U. S. S. Hannibal* spent forty-two years in the service, twenty-eight of them in charting the Caribbean and the Pacific approaches to Panama, most vital position in our system of sea defense. During this period, the *Hannibal* produced seventy charts for the naval service, covering every possible obstruction to ships and recording all depths, just as an automobile map might tell you how far it was to the next bump, turn, or detour. The *Hannibal* has been retired after long and fruitful service, and no one knows how many vessels she has saved by her scientific intellect. Her successor, the *Bowditch*, continues this valuable service to sailing men.

When Ships of the Fleet Are Close to One Another, They Often Communicate by Means of Flag Signalmen

In National Emergencies, Many Experienced Officers of the Merchant Marine Join the Navy

12 *OUR MERCHANT MARINE*

THE NAVY has been interested throughout its history in the development and maintenance of a strong merchant service. During the nineteenth century, from the time of the speedy clipper ships, American bottoms were the envy of the world, but in the twentieth century, the increase in the American standard of living and wages of labor made it difficult for American shippers to compete with the low scales of pay in foreign services. The United States Maritime Commission, under the leadership of Admiral Emory S. Land, a regular naval officer, did much to put the United States Flag back on the sea lanes of the world. The Navy is indebted to the whole merchant service for this rise in our fortunes at sea.

In time of stress the Navy can call on the Merchant Marine for assistance in ships and men. It has long been a policy to build into merchantmen those ship characteristics that will make them easily convertible to naval auxiliaries. Tankers, transports, mine layers and sweepers, supply ships, and cargo vessels of all kinds are some of the auxiliaries of the fleet which the Navy obtains direct from the Merchant Marine in periods of expansion.

The Merchant Marine Reserve is part of the Naval Reserve, and when you sail in an American ship the chances are very good that your "skipper" and his first officer and the chief engineer are also officers in the Naval Reserve. When the Navy takes over merchant ships, these officers are taken over with them in most cases. Having been trained in naval lore, they are ready for convoy duty, for work on auxiliaries of the fleet, and for other special assignments.

The Navy maintains a school for Merchant Marine officers in its receiving ship at New York, where between runs, or when not on regular schedules at sea, they may receive advanced courses in naval warfare. Merchant Marine officers are invaluable to the Navy, as are thousands of their seamen, because of their long experience on the ocean lanes and knowledge of seamanship, engineering, storage of cargo, and ship handling in all kinds of weather.

The Navy Looks to the Merchant Marine for Many of the Men Needed to Man Its Growing Fleet

A "Battle Wagon" Is Launched after Its Many Months on the Ways

13 BUILDING A SHIP OF THE LINE

WHEN the American people are asked to spend $75,000,000 for the building of a battleship, they have a right to know what they are getting for their money and why it costs so much. That is a long and interesting story.

A great ship passes through many stages from the time of its conception until it actually joins the fleet, ready to take its place in the battle line. First of all, after the money has been made available by Congress, the Navy's Bureau of Construction and Repair co-operates with the General Board of the Navy in making a large number of designs, calculations, and drawings. These drawings present different specifications for the gun power, speed, armor, and other characteristics of the ship. After much deliberation among the experts in engineering, ordnance, and shipbuilding, the main features of the new ship are agreed upon. The length, beam, draft, freeboard, armor thickness, location and size of turrets and guns, weight of machinery, and cruising radius are specified.

For the *North Carolina* and *Washington*, the newest battleships, this mental work required more than a year of the best efforts of hundreds of men, and the final decisions were the results of more than seventy separate studies in design. This long period of planning is necessary because, before the keel of such an expensive ship is laid, the Navy must be certain that the ship will be the best in her class when she is finished. If her normal life is to be, say, twenty-five years, in her twenty-fourth year she must be still a good fighter in relation to ships of newer design that are younger. Thus the *West Virginia*, the last battleship built before the Washington Disarmament Conference in 1922, compares favorably in performance with the latest designs, because careful thought was given to her construction before her keel was laid.

The second step is the preparation of plans based on the design selected. This ordinarily takes several months, and is so complete that Navy Yard or private ship-building experts can study them, make detailed estimates for material and labor costs, and for its construction. Bids are invited, three additional months generally being given to bidders to prepare their estimates. After the contract is awarded, the

This Anti-aircraft Gun Is Only One of the Hundreds of Complicated Mechanisms
to Be Found on the Navy's Ships

real work on the detailed design begins. About 500 draftsmen are needed to develop the 5,000 preliminary plans, to which 5,000 other plans are added as construction progresses.

Construction material for the hull must be purchased first. This is special high quality steel which takes a long time to manufacture. Since there are few armor manufacturers, armor-plate orders also must be placed early. Before the keel is laid, 1,500 tons of structural material should be ready, so that work will not be delayed. The ceremony of laying the keel is always attended by representatives, usually including the Governor, of the State for which the ship is named.

Shipfitters and shipwrights do the early construction. These men, who are among the mechanical workers so necessary to the national defense, consist of loftsmen, fitters, drillers, calkers, riveters, welders, and machine operators.

The ship is built on a slanting way so that it can be easily launched. Therefore proper alignment of each piece of material is vital. As the work progresses, machinists align the engine foundation and other equipment, the boilermaker does the same for the boilers, and the pipefitter, the sheet-metal worker, and the electrician all come aboard to do their special jobs. Small boats for the battleship, such as barges, gigs, motor boats, dinghies, and whaleboats are all begun. The pattern shop, the forge, and woodworking shops keep busy at their respective tasks of preparing materials for castings that are turned out in the foundry.

One of the most difficult jobs to be done is the design and construction of turrets. It involves close fits, so that the turret may withstand the severe jolts it gets when the big guns are firing and recoiling. The rotating parts alone of each turret weigh approximately 1,500 tons — the average weight of a destroyer. Turrets are constructed on concrete platforms to insure accuracy of measurements. When the turret is complete, rotating cranes lift them into the ship.

When the battleship is sixty or seventy per cent complete, it is ready for launching. This major event occurs almost two years after the keel has been laid, and the greatest ceremony of all now takes place. Crowds gather, pennants flutter, and the sponsor stands ready to christen the ship.

Many calculations have been made to effect the perfect launching, for there are dangerous possibilities when a huge mass of thousands of tons is sent sliding down the ways. Launching a vessel is the most exciting and critical moment of her entire construction. Naval constructors, engineers, and their hundreds of helpers who are responsible for the transfer of the hull from dry land to water will not feel easy until the task is successfully accomplished.

After launching, the battleship is secured alongside the dock. Now the side armor, turrets, guns, and superstructure are installed. And then the vessel at last is delivered, and is ready to be commissioned. Officers and crew are assembled and the vessel is officially taken over.

After the final touches have been put on the ship, and after supplies have been loaded, the battleship takes her preliminary trials. These are followed by a "shakedown" cruise, so that all hands may become familiar with their duties, try out the machinery, and test the turrets and guns. After this cruise, official trials are run, and the Board of Inspection and Survey from the Navy Department watch every detail of the craft's performance. Fuel consumption, speed, and propeller revolutions are recorded, so that her standards may be set.

Upon completion of these trials, the ship is ready to join the fleet. Everything that skilled craftsmen can do to assure her a successful, happy life has been done.

Every Fighting Unit of the Navy, from Battleships to the Torpedo Planes Shown Here,
Is a Triumph of Mechanical Ingenuity

Destroyers Lay a Smoke Screen to Hide the Main Battle Line

14 A MODERN NAVAL ENGAGEMENT

Now THAT we are acquainted with the men, the ships, the planes, and other parts of our Navy, just how do they operate in battle? How would they defend us against a big enemy fleet approaching our shores? In what order would the ships meet the enemy to give him the maximum punishment? What tactics would be used? By what strategy would the commanders of our fleet finally gain the upper hand and force the hostile fleet to strike its colors — or go to the bottom?

Let us send our fleet against an imaginary foe and see what happens.

A big enemy fleet — a force of battleships, cruisers, destroyers, submarines, and aircraft carriers, with a train of repair and supply ships in its wake — is plowing through the ocean toward our shores. The intention of the commanders of this threatening armada is to engage the United States Fleet and, by sinking or damaging most of it, to crack our first line of defense hopelessly. Once that grim work has been accomplished, the preliminaries to a mass invasion can begin. Our merchant

70

shipping along American coasts will be at the mercy of enemy raiders, and our sea trade will halt. Key points along our shores will be surprised and seized by hostile landing parties. The bombing of our coastal cities, and even cities hundreds of miles inland, by planes based on enemy aircraft carriers and seized bases, will get under way. Our country will be surrounded by an iron ring of ships — and the iron ring will begin to close in earnest with the landing of hordes of enemy troops and equipment at points already captured and prepared.

So the enemy thinks. For years he has planned it. Nothing has been left to chance. Every one of his fighting ships is prepared for the initial job of breaking and scattering our fleet. And already, on their mission of destruction, his ships are entering American waters.

The United States Navy, however, has not been caught napping. It too has made plans, has developed secret weapons, has worked out an elaborate strategy of defense. Already, in fact, by its world-wide system of communications, it knows the enemy is on the way — knows the formation and strength of his forces — and is waiting for him. Every man in our fleet, ready at his post, is resolved to sink or capture the hostile armada before it comes anywhere near American soil.

Planes from our aircraft carriers and island strongholds, racing far out to sea, have just located the oncoming fleet and have radioed in to our ships its exact position, the speed with which it is traveling toward our shores, and its true compass course. The Commander-in-Chief of the United States Fleet now endeavors to maneuver our forces so that contact will come at a time and place most advantageous for his ships. The strength of the wind, the weather, the state of the sea, the position of the sun in relation to the two forces when actual contact is made — all enter into his advance calculations.

At last the zero hour for action approaches. The enemy has been sighted. In the turrets, at the broadside guns, on the anti-aircraft platforms, on the bridge, in the engine rooms, every one is on edge, tense and ready. Powder and shell are up, decks are stripped for action.

Enemy aircraft from opposing carriers are sighted, and our own aircraft take off from carrier flight decks to meet them above and under the clouds. Now they are in a dogfight over our own battle line, horizontal bombers and dive bombers, trying to get in position to hit, and being beaten off by our own fighter planes and anti-aircraft fire. Above the opposing fleet there is similar action, and unless our planes are better equipped, have stronger gun power and greater speed, our victory may be seriously imperiled before a single big gun is fired by one side or the other.

Meanwhile shells and powder continue to move up to the turrets from the handling rooms, and range finders bear on the enemy. Opening ranges are decided upon after allowing for atmospheric conditions. To the plotting rooms below decks, spotters in the "tops" transmit over telephones, through voice tubes, or by visual signals the range of the enemy. The big guns are elevated; pointers and trainers inside the turrets find their targets.

Suddenly a great roar marks the firing of the opening salvos from the entire fleet. Aircraft spotters high in the air radio back where the shells have struck, what kind of pattern the falling shells formed — over, under, or straddling the ships of the enemy. Calculations are checked with the spotters aboard each ship, and in less than half a minute the second salvos are fired on a new range, up or down, to effect hits.

Two hits are reported on the number 3 ship in the enemy line, and two battleships of our fleet concentrate on the struck ship to put it out of action as soon as possible. Meanwhile the number 6 ship in our own fleet has been hit near the waterline under number 1 turret, and a burst in the handling room has put the

Submarines Can Dive Quickly, Creep up on Enemy Ships, and Launch Their Torpedoes with Deadly Effect — Unless the Enemy's Destroyers Are Too Alert for Them

The Diminutive "Mosquito Boat" Can Often Dash Among Enemy Ships, Get a Hit with One of Its Torpedoes, and Flee before the Enemy Can Retaliate

turret out of action and killed many of the crew. We can now expect the enemy in his turn to try to follow up his initial success by finishing off this ship.

But now a group of enemy destroyers is seen approaching from the rear of our fleet to try to lay down a torpedo barrage. Our own cruisers and destroyers sally forth to engage them, sink them, or turn them back.

The third salvos from our battleships are now striking with telling effect, and the number 3 ship of the enemy is on fire and leaving the battle line — falling back to where she will become the prey of our submarines, planes, and destroyers. Six minutes later, enemy destroyers are seen to be laying down a smoke screen in front of the struck ship.

The opposing battle line has now shifted its course, and has decided to increase the range in an attempt to throw our guns off their deadly aim. There is a delay in the firing from both fleets until the new ranges are determined.

"Spots" come in from our scouts and are checked with the range-finder readings on the American flagship. Another salvo booms out. It falls short; but the enemy, firing within seconds of our own salvos, scores a hit near the bridge of the number 2 vessel in our battle line.

Aboard this ship there is momentary chaos. Many on the bridge have been killed and wounded, and are being carried below to a dressing station. The steering gear having been wrecked, the ship falls out of line, and the order goes out to "con" (steer) from the after station. The effect of the enemy shell burst has also jammed the number 2 turret roller paths, so that the turret cannot continue firing.

From the after steering station, the struck ship is soon put under control and resumes her position in the battle line. But the enemy is concentrating fire now on this ship and pours two more hits into her armor belt, one of which bursts in the forward fire room.

Meanwhile American gunnery also is proving its worth — striking the foe with telling effect from all along our battle line. Two more ships of the enemy have been forced to leave the battle and fall behind, with our destroyers and cruisers in hot pursuit, attempting to finish them off with torpedoes and gunfire. Enemy destroyers engage them in turn, hoping to save their own ships from final destruction.

In the air, American fighter squadrons have gained control, and have forced down into the sea thirty enemy bombers and fighters.

Destroyers, Like Submarines, Are Always Ready to Greet the Enemy With Torpedoes

Destroyers Make a Sudden Change of Course While Screening Aircraft Carriers
and Battleships in Maneuvers

But now things are happening so fast it is impossible to record them. The enemy line turns away 39 degrees to escape the murderous fire of our guns, but our Commander-in-Chief follows this move with a similar one, hoping to keep the range and fire three times every minute. He succeeds, and American gunnery keeps the upper hand — two of the enemy battleships are listing heavily, and another is foundering. Dive and horizontal bombers concentrate on these ships, seeking to sink them.

As the punishing salvos continue, there is a collision between two ships of the enemy, both vitally injured and out of control from gunfire. American destroyers close in at 40 knots and let go their torpedoes, forcing what is left of the enemy battle line to shift its course to escape being hit.

Two more salvos and the last three ships of the foreign fleet are seen to be going down. But they do not strike their flags. A last salvo is fired from one of them just before her guns are awash, and she goes down fighting. Hundreds of men are in the water as another ship blows up from fires started in her magazines.

The battle is decided, but two of our own ships have been sunk, and three are listing heavily. The rescue of our own men and those of the enemy by destroyers and cruisers has already begun.

Twelve ships of the enemy have been sunk; three more are sinking. Enemy de-

75

stroyers and cruisers have left the scene of action and are steaming away over the horizon. They are all that is left of the enemy force, and our own speed demons are in pursuit and hope to catch up to them before nightfall.

Thus American seapower has met the supreme challenge, but only because of superior training and better marksmanship. Had not every unit been able to work as a team, the battle would not have been won. Had there not been constant target practices at all ranges, in all kinds of weather, our men would not have been ready. They have met and defeated the enemy only because the citizens of the United States have seen fit to give their Navy the best in men, guns, and ammunition. Years of training; efficient ship and aircraft builders; inventors; bolt-factory workers in Milwaukee; a propeller manufacturer in Texas — all of American industry has contributed to this battle, and what they have done has achieved the result.